The BATHTUB

The BATHTUB

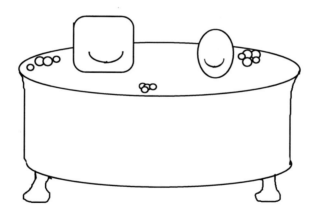

A Perspective on
Marriage & Divorce

Katherine Obermeyer

Copyright © 2011 by Katherine Obermeyer.

Library of Congress Control Number: 2011918678
ISBN: Hardcover 978-1-4653-8166-8
Softcover 978-1-4653-8165-1
Ebook 978-1-4653-8167-5

All rights reserved. No part of this book may be reproduced or transmitted in any form or by any means, electronic or mechanical, including photocopying, recording, or by any information storage and retrieval system, without permission in writing from the copyright owner.

This book was printed in the United States of America.

To order additional copies of this book, contact:
Xlibris Corporation
1-888-795-4274
www.Xlibris.com
Orders@Xlibris.com

Contents

X & Y—Stories 11

The Bathtub of Marriage and
    Divorce 35
        Love and Courting 36
        Marriage 37
        Natural Cooling of Water 39
        Rotting the Floor 40
        Perfect Balance 41
        Get Out Before You Fall 42
        Get Out and Leave 43
        Unfair Division of Labor 46
        Playing Around—Splashing 48
        Open Marriage 51
        Playing Around with Money 53
        Ice 55
        Hot Water 57
        Kids 58
        Thoughts to Ponder 63

How to Make a Marriage Work 68
        1. Whose marriage is this? 68
        2. Water will get cold. 70
        3. So how do you add warm water? 71
        4. Overflow—do you have an overflow drain line? 72
        5. Learn how to drain water. 74
        6. When ice chunks fall into your tub,
           huddle together 79
        7. Don't let anyone add burning hot water ... 83
        8. What about when someone you love rages
           at the universe (or worse, at you)? 85
        9. Some people just don't look at divorce as an
           option 87
        10. Staying together for the kids? 93
        11. Homework 94

Dedicated to
all those who value
their marriage.

Preface

What really matters, when we think about our lives, is our relationships with each other.

The marital relationship is unique because we choose to marry.

Each marriage is supposed to last until someone dies.

X & Y—Stories

X and Y sort of fell into a bathtub.

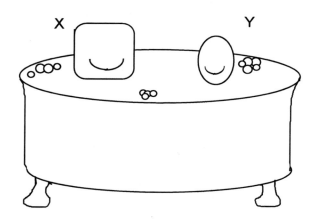

How did they really get there? It is a mystery.

What we know is that all of a sudden, there they were.

They were sitting in a warm bubble bath, just listening to the bubbles pop.

One of them said, "This feels really great." The other said, "I've never been in a bathtub that was so warm and wonderful. I just love it here."

It felt so good and seemed so right that they decided to stay, together, in the bathtub, forever. (He asked her to marry him—and she said yes.)

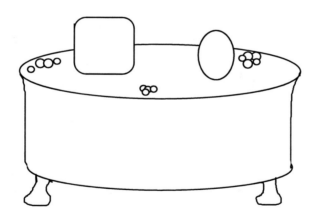

X and Y got married.

The Bathtub

Choosing to marry was like choosing to stay in the bathtub. The two people in the bathtub are the only people in the bathtub. It is their marriage.

People wondered, *Were they nervous?* A little. *Did they wonder what life would bring?* Of course. All of us wonder what will happen in the future.

But they were certain it would be OK for them because it felt so right.

The Bathtub

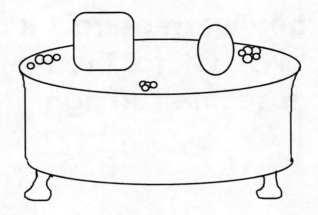

Time went by.

The Bathtub

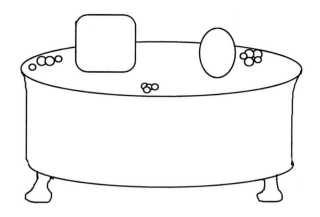

Life went on.

They moved in together. They went to work when they needed to. They made decisions about what to buy. Sometimes, they even fought a little.

Life went on and on, and

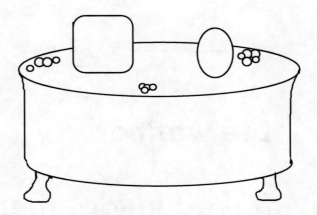

do you know what happened?

The Bathtub

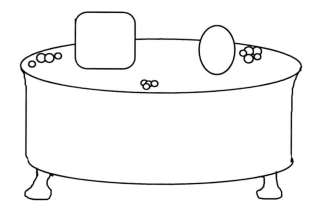

Not much.

The Bathtub

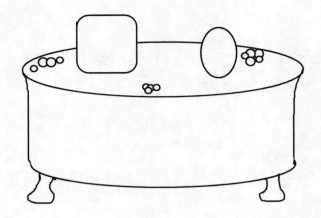

Well, unless you count this:

When X thought about their marriage, she thought—well, we don't know what she thought because she didn't talk about it a lot. She was so

The Bathtub

busy I couldn't quite tell if she thought about it at all.

And Y was the same way.

So over time, like all bathtubs, the water cooled off.

And that is how a whole bunch of marriages fail. Nobody really did anything wrong. But as anyone who has taken a bath knows, water cools. And eventually, the water gets cold.

(Well, unless you learn to add more warm water.)

So some people would just wonder, *What happened to the love?*

The Bathtub

Why doesn't our water feel warm anymore?

Most people don't bring it up because they think it is just them.

"I am not feeling very warm. I must need to do something else," and one day,

Y asked X for a divorce. "I don't think it matters whether we stay

together or not. What I know is that I don't want to stay in this cold water with you any longer. I am leaving," and he left.

X was sitting in the bathtub. The water was cold. She had choices, but I don't think she saw them. What she said to me was "Do you remember when the water was so warm, it felt so right and Y was still here?" She was sad and missed Y. But then after a while, I heard that she said, "I am so angry at Y. How could he leave me here in this cold water? It is really cold in here."

It got really bad when she saw Y in the store with X2. Y said, "How are you doing? This is X2. X2 and I are getting married. We feel warm water all around us."

How could Y decide to get in another bathtub? she thought.

Why was the water warm for X2 and Y when it was so cold for X?

And just so you know, I'll tell you.

Y left the bathtub. He got out, which was hard, but

he remembered how cold it was and just couldn't live that way. Life is too short to freeze the rest of your life.

He dried off. And put some clothes on. And he felt warmer after a while.

Then one day, he met X2 and she told him a joke. They went out for dinner and a movie

The Bathtub

(which he hadn't done for a while); and then, *bam*, he realized he had fallen into a bathtub with X2.

It was different than when Y was young and with X. But it reminded him of that. He felt younger, and it felt so good to be warm again. So he was pretty happy with it.

The Bathtub

X and Y had friends.

Here is the story of X and Y. (I know it is sometimes hard to tell the difference, but truly each story is unique.)

X and Y started out in a similar way. They fell into the bathtub with nice warm water and lots of fun bubbles. They liked being there together and decided to make it permanent.

It was a pretty good life, well, if you didn't notice that every once in a while, Y would splash a little.
Y would cover it up by shouting something and then splashing. Lots of times he would say, "Look over there," and X would look; and then he would splash and hope she missed it. Y was really just playing around—if you know what I mean.

X did miss it a lot. I'm actually not sure she noticed.

The Bathtub

So this splashing went on, and there was water on the floor. Y was pretending he hadn't splashed, and X didn't notice he was splashing.

Which just meant that there was water on the floor.

No one mopped it up.

At first, of course, this doesn't mean much. It doesn't seem to be doing any harm.

But it is. Of course, this is why parents all over the world nag at their kids to wipe up the water on the floor or not to splash out of the bathtub. Most people dry off in the bathtub so they don't get the floor very wet.

Because if you don't mop up the water on the floor, eventually, the floor rots. The bathtub floor gets wet, and the boards that are supporting the bathtub rot.

The Bathtub

Sometimes people notice this rotten floor. Y noticed the rotten floor but just kept splashing. You see, it took so long for the floor to rot, that he was in the habit of splashing and just couldn't figure out how his life would be any fun at all if he couldn't splash some.
X was nervous. "Was the bathtub going to fall through the floor?" X tiptoed around the bathtub. Maybe if she didn't make any sudden moves, the bathtub would stay where it was.

Have you seen people do this? I've seen whole groups of people tiptoe around, not bringing up topics in the hope that the bathtub won't fall through the floor.

That lasted for a while.

But really, eventually, X wondered, *What is causing the floor to rot?*

X started to pay attention to the little things. And one day, X discovered that Y was splashing.

The Bathtub

Was X mad? Whew—she was seething. "You mean to tell me that you think this splashing is just for fun? That it doesn't affect the foundation of our bathtub? That I should just ignore it? What do you think will happen? Don't you see that the bathtub is going to fall someday?"

But Y didn't see it; Y had been splashing for years and just distracting X. So Y thought he could do the same thing now.

"Now X, honey, don't get all mad about this splashing—it just doesn't mean anything to me like you mean to me. You know that. I'll stop if you want me to."

But Y had no intention to actually stop; he just said that because it was what X wanted to hear, and he knew it.

X thought about just getting out of the bathtub and leaving Y. Should she? She promised to stay in the bathtub, but Y promised not to splash around.

The Bathtub

What really bothered her was that when she talked about it, she found out that we all knew already. Some of us thought she was just ignoring it because their bathtub was in their nice house, and Y provided the money for the house. Some of us thought she just didn't want to know. Some of us had thought about telling her.

She couldn't believe that she was the last person to find out. Of course, she wasn't actually the last person to find out. But she wouldn't realize that unless she started talking about it with others. Then she would find out that not everyone knew.

It made her very depressed and sad.

She thought about her life. She didn't think she could ever find another bathtub that would be warm like the one she had with Y. He said he would stop. She decided to give Y another chance.

The Bathtub

But she paid more attention.

And pretty soon she found out that he was still splashing.

So she got out of the bathtub.

You should have seen Y a little while after X left. I don't think anyone knew, but X was adding warm water all the time. So without X, the water got cold.

Y knew the water was cold, and he didn't really understand why because he never noticed what it was that X did to make it warm.

Y sat there in the bathtub alone and cold. He realized that the splashing wasn't very much fun without the bathtub of warm water.

He missed the bathtub of warm water.

The Bathtub of Marriage and Divorce

I sat in the bathtub one morning and listened to the bubbles pop. I felt the water cool. I realized that this was just like marriage.

How we treat each other in our daily lives is what makes a loving, lasting relationship. Perhaps this book can help be a way to find distance and clarity to understand and solve individual problems that add up to a marriage in trouble. Let's look at the individual people in unique situations and try to hold to guiding principles that define a morality of trust.

A friend pointed out to me that you can see this also if you just drink a cup of coffee. Pour the hot coffee. Is it too hot? Wait for it to cool some. After a while, it is perfect. After more time, it is cold and not as good as it was.

The natural cooling is rather like gravity: it just happens.

Love and Courting

Sometimes love is like being in a bathtub. You are in the bathtub with the person you love. The bathtub is fun!

You find that, suddenly, life is different. Bubbles pop all around. You notice how the temperature is just right. You are more comfortable than you have been with anyone else. You and your bath buddy are amazingly compatible. You both feel good. You may even decide that this is it. This is the one. You will marry this bathtub buddy.

Marriage

Marriage is like this bathtub that you are in. The two of you view the world differently than everyone else. You have joined together and are your own bath group.

You remain two individual people, but you have this bathtub. Surrounded by warm water, you share this just with your spouse.

Have you ever heard the best way to clean a bathtub is to get in? You can reach all the sides; you are not leaning across. You don't mind getting water on your elbow because you are naked and in the water. It is good to be in clean water, in a clean tub. Life seems calm at that moment. It is very tempting to just sit back and enjoy it.

Natural Cooling of Water

Some people are better at working at their marriage. If no one does anything, eventually, the water will cool off and you will start to feel cold. The bath will cool off on its own. It isn't any fun to be in a cold marriage.

Sometimes it is just that simple. Some marriages break up because no one did anything, and it just grew too cold.

Let's call the cold relationship failure of marriage the natural tendency of water to cool off.

This is why premarriage counseling talks about working

at your marriage. You need to watch it. What temperature is it? Should someone do something like add warm water?

Rotting the Floor

After time, adding warm water will fill the bathtub. Have you added too much water and need to drain some out? Someone will have to take this action or the bath will overflow. Since the bathtub just has two people in it, that someone is either you or your spouse. Water that overflows will ruin the carpet/tile/linoleum and rot the floor underneath the bathtub. This is a marriage where people worked at it, but they didn't realize all the different types of work that needed to be done. They were able to add water and keep themselves warm, but they were unable to drain the water out or mop up the outside when water overflowed.

Eventually, the bathtub will fall through the floor. Of course, when a bathtub falls through the floor, people are going to be hurt.

Perfect Balance

Really, there is the time when these people will sense that the floor is getting soft. They will stop moving around. "Don't move because too much motion may cause the floor to give."

People tiptoe around and try to perfectly balance each other in an attempt to delay the inevitable crashing through the floor, the painful break-up of the bathtub (marriage).

This works for a while. How old are you? If you are terminally ill, this may work. But for people younger than eighty-five, this doesn't work. But people try it.

Get Out Before You Fall

Some people get divorced if they feel like the bathtub is going to fall through the floor.

Deciding to get out is really a rational decision. Why fall together through the hole and risk breaking their necks? But that is only one possible choice. Why not remodel? Why not do what is needed to repair the floor foundation?

Get Out and Leave

If the decision is to get out of the bathtub, then the important point is that both people get out. Sometimes one person gets out—"Look at the floor! It is going to fall! I'm leaving!" (Very dramatic.) If the other person just starts crying, remembering when this bathtub was warm and comfortable and doesn't get out, then this person will still fall through the floor, just by themselves. This is the sad "divorce didn't solve any problems for me" victim attitude. It doesn't help. Though the crash now only affects one person, that person experiences it alone. This person is most likely to lie in the broken bathtub when they land.

"Look, my leg is broken. I remember back before the bathtub fell through the floor. I remember when the bathtub was warm and my bath buddy was with me. Oh, I'd rather be there than here."

To deny the current situation and

live in the past does not help fix anything. It just prolongs the problem.

If the people get the floor fixed and learn how to keep the floor dry, then they have an even better relationship.

If people haven't learned some way to prevent the rotting of the floor, then they are likely to damage their new floor too. When that happens, they normally just get out and proceed into another bathtub with the same problems.

It may not be the bathtub itself that is the problem. It may be that until you learn how to handle the water, each relationship you have will have problems thriving. Deal with the issue—fix your relationship behavior.

Unfair Division of Labor

"I can't believe you didn't mop up the water. I told you to mop up the water."

This failure of marriage is particularly sad because it is so avoidable. If you notice water on the floor, why tell someone else to mop it up? Why not just mop it up yourself? But sometimes people act like this: "We agreed mopping was your job. I'm over here adding warm water, just like we agreed, and you are there not mopping it up. You just aren't helping. I cannot stand it. The floor will rot and I'm getting out this time. I'm not fixing the floor again. I just can't do it all. You never help."

Normally, the person who failed to mop up the water had reasons for not doing it. These are reasons like "I was too busy supporting us financially. I didn't notice when the water overflowed." Or even sometimes "When you yell at me to mop it up, I won't. You need to learn to ask me nicely."
If you drain some water, then the water may not overflow.

Playing Around—Splashing

Have you seen a marriage with one person adding warm water and draining water and the other person splashing water?
The continuous splashing of water over the edge causes water on the floor. The floor will rot, eventually, if the first person keeps the water warm and everyone stays in the tub. Normally, this is not what happens. One person is working at the marriage, adding water, draining water, and the other person is playing around, splashing the water out. Maybe at the beginning the working-at-the-marriage person may not notice how the water is getting

The Bathtub

on the floor and just mop it up. But there comes a day when this person finds out it is due to the other person. Then they either get out of the bathtub or they start mopping.

Getting out sounds like this "I can't believe you did this to me. Here I was in the bathtub, draining water, adding warm water, and you deliberately splashed water on the floor. Don't you know that this will cause the floor to rot and the bathtub to fall? I am leaving. I will find someone else to be in the bathtub with."

Sometimes the person just adds mopping to their list. They are now the "draining water, adding water, and mopping the floor" person. They may even lower the level of the water in the bathtub so that it is harder to splash out of the tub. This you can recognize. It looks like going on the business trips with your spouse, taking dinner to the office, keeping tabs on the other person. It means less availability and time for the other person to cheat.

Of course, sometimes the person splashing can be trained to mop it up. Or the person calms down and stops splashing. These both can save the marriage.

Which one will happen? What

factors decide that? Mainly we're told that it is how the working-at-the-marriage person reacts and how the splashing person perceives this reaction.

Sometimes the splashing inspires nagging. Nagging to mop it up leads to rebellion to splash more and not mop up at all. Neither one mops, and either the water all splashes out, one person leaves, both people leave, or the eventual rotting of the floor causes the bathtub to fall and crack, sometimes throwing both people out of the bathtub.

Open Marriage

Open marriage is when the

water is drained out and no more water is added. With no water, the other person can't splash. Decide that it is okay. Share the adventure. The floor won't rot, and everything is ok. It isn't as comfortable as being in a warm bath.

People may stay in a dry bathtub, but it takes a blanket or a room that is warm enough. Otherwise, everyone just gets cold and, eventually, has to get out to get warm. This is a cold way to live, but it does work. The bitter laugh, the knowing look, the skepticism in this marriage is the temperature of the air.

Playing Around with Money

Some people cheat sexually; some people cheat financially. When you make decisions for the other person or make decisions without the other person's consent, you are breaking the marriage bond. You are either splashing water out or dumping in ice cold water. If two people share a goal, and one person makes decisions that bring them farther and farther from the goal, it won't help how the marriage feels. Examples of this are easy to spot. This looks like new clothes, new cars, sports equipment, jewelry, remodeling the house, buying a fifth wheel—

any expense that is for one person that benefits one of the two people in the marriage.

The key to this is getting the other person's input and listening. Either convincing them, compromising with them, or somehow arranging a deal.

To lie, steal, or hide the truth is like taking a big bucket and dumping water on the floor. Though your spouse may not notice right away, you have just weakened the boards supporting your tub.

Ice

Sometimes life just dumps ice in your bathtub. We've all seen this. It looks like the death of a child, life-changing financial loss, argument over politics due to an event, or even a tragedy like a flood, earthquake, fire or mudslide. Sometimes it is just the demands of life, the children's needs that never stop, or just a stepchild—any sort of turmoil that comes into the house.

Though some couples work together and bond in crisis, others withdraw from the pain and get out of the icy or cold water. The thing about cold water is that, many times, it is no one's fault. Many times the water gets icy just because of life. Life happens.

Think about two people in a bathtub. Dump ice in the center of the tub with them. Do they huddle together and turn on the warm water? Or do they move away from the ice, to the edges, and as the water gets colder, do they just stay there because crossing the icy center to the other person is overwhelming? Do they hope that their end of the bathtub will just warm up? Because we know that it won't. Not on its own. And even if you start adding warm water, it takes a while to get through the ice in the center. The person on the other end is just going to feel cold. For quite some time.

Your best defense against this failure of marriage is to hang out close together. Then when ice comes in, you are not caught apart. Don't let yourselves live on the opposite ends of the tub.

Hot Water

Sometimes the water may get hot. Ever heard of people in "hot water"?

Hot water is very uncomfortable. People get burned and get out very quickly. No one can stay in the water if it gets too hot.

What does this look like? Hot water is when everyone feels the consequences of your actions. Think about bankruptcy, infidelity—a situation in which the other person has no choice but to take some kind of action. In hot water, the other person is forced to do something. They may not want to, but they have no choice, especially in burning hot water. It will burn. People will move. They cannot do anything else.

Kids

Children are born in the bathtub. Well, some children are born in the bathtub. Some children are born from parents who feel the warm water of love. These children are in the bathtub with their parents. Children sometimes see what is happening in the bathtub. Mostly, though, kids don't know any better and think whatever the bathtub situation they are in is just how it is. They don't know what it felt like when the bathtub was warm years ago. They just know how it is now, and think this is normal.

So the water may cool off and no one warms it. The child will just think water is cool. They may not remember feeling any warm water.

Or the water may be drained

out, and everyone is cold.

Or they may watch one parent draining, adding water, and mopping up the floor; and the other person is splashing. They just think this is normal.

When bathtubs fall through the floor, everyone falls. The parents AND the children fall. This can get pretty ugly.

Sometimes the parents feel the cold water, but don't know how to warm it up. They want to get out, but stay in the bathtub "for the children."

Lately, a lot of parents get out and find another bathtub with another person. The children move from bathtub to bathtub each week. Children are very resilient and get used to this. Children who adapt well may form a larger bathtub in their mind in which all of the people live. Of course, depending on what skills the people have, it may be warm at one end and cold at the other.

The single divorced parent may still be in the old tub, or they may have gotten out. Some kids grow up outside the tub (not in a marriage). If there is no tub, the important message is that you are still an independent family.

Children in a marriage with hot

water get burned. Sometimes burns take years to heal. How long it takes to heal depends on how long everyone stays in the hot water and what kind of treatment they get when they get out.

Staying in a marriage with really hot water for the kids' sake is a mistake. Everyone gets burned. No one is comfortable, and it just doesn't work.

If you want to stay in the bathtub for the kids' sake, then you need to learn to warm the water, to drain the water, and to mop up any water that is splashed.

If the floor is already rotten, then for the kids' sake, you need to get out and repair the floor, then get everyone back in.

Thoughts to Ponder

What is the water? How do you know what temperature water you are adding? Or are you not even adding any water?

How do you let go—or drain the water?

Can one person drain and add water? Or will it overflow unless both people drain and add water?

What does it mean to mop up

the water?

Can you list five ways of splashing over the tub? What is the tub?

Why do people get in the bathtub?

If the water is colder, is it natural cooling or was cold water or ice added? Can you tell?

Can having a baby build a bathtub and fill it with warm water?

What causes the water to cool off slowly or quickly?

Can a lot of sex keep the water

warm without adding any warm water?

When someone is adding water that is too hot, what should you do? What if it is you? What if it is your bath buddy?

Can kids splash too much—more than the parents can fill it up?

When someone dies and they leave the bathtub, what happens to the other person? After the person is gone, do you crawl back in the bathtub and try to keep it warm? Or do you bravely go into the world?

Where do you go if you're not in a bathtub of love? Are you in the air? What is air?

The newly remodeled bathroom rarely looks like the old bathroom.

The complexity of the scenarios is why people can't categorize why marriages fail. It can easily be a combination of reasons in any particular marriage.

Is nagging just adding cold water?

Sometimes people struggle with this idea:
"What do you mean the bathtub is like a marriage? We're not wet, and we go other places without each other.

Marriage isn't a trap."

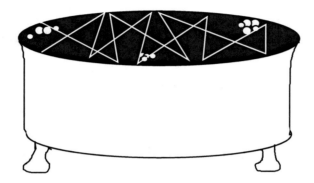

This is a marriage trap. They do exist, but it isn't the definition of marriage; it is just, sometimes, the bathtub has bars across the top and is full of sticky black stuff. You need to make sure that this is not what you have BEFORE you get in. Folks that step into this trap normally do it in a rush and don't take the time to learn about their marriage before they get in.

Are you wondering if you should marry and asking your family and friends what they think? That can mean that you are sensing a trap that will take away your enjoyment of life. Most people I've seen that enjoyed being married wanted to get married and they knew it. They would even stand up for it. They would let others delay it, but not call it off. Are you in love?

How to Make a Marriage Work

1. Whose marriage is this?
Who is in the marriage? Sometimes folks get confused by these questions. The first step in marriage is realizing who owns the marriage, who has a say in decisions, and who gets a vote.

The Christian religion sums up this point by saying "The man and woman leave their families and the two become one."

The only two people in the bathtub are you and your fiancée or spouse. A marriage is just two people.

No one else gets a vote. No one. Sometimes folks talk about a three-way deal—you, your spouse, and God. Is God everywhere, and is the deal really you and God? The answer to this is simple. If you see God in you or your spouse sees

God in them, THEN you will see God as a part of the bathtub. If you don't see God, you won't see God in the bathtub. Does that matter? Depends on how you would answer this question: Would you change what you do if you knew God was watching? If you would, then it would matter in your life.

But the message here isn't that you need, or don't need, to look for God in your marriage. The message here is that the bathtub doesn't include your family, friends, neighbors, or coworkers. **It is just two people.**

This is important, because this alone can cause marriages to fail. People tend to reach out and talk about the bad stuff. "Then, what did he say?" We don't share the good stuff. So, it is a problem that sometimes our support network encourages us to leave, just because of the one-sided info they get.

The Bathtub

2. Water will get cold.

Most people like a nice warm bath. They get in and sigh. "Awww—this feels so good to sit here in this warm water. I will lean back and enjoy this moment."

And they close their eyes and sit in the water.

And the water cools off.

If you don't do anything, your marriage can fail. Most premarriage counseling warns people to work at their marriage. Normally, they are pretty vague at what kind of work this is. They just say "marriage takes work." Spend time on your relationship.

Time isn't the problem or the answer. What matters is what is making you feel like this is where you want to be. And it isn't the tub. And it isn't the faucets. Sometimes people think it could be the location of the house in which the bathtub resides.

Really, it is the warm water. Warm water is why you feel okay sitting there naked. Warm water is why you want to stay.

When the water gets cold, you want to get out.

3. So how do you add warm water? What makes you or your spouse feel good? Feeling respect, admiration, physical love. Expressing love in the ways that you recognize or your spouse recognizes is adding warm water.

This looks like listening to the other person. Look at the other person. At the beginning, people tend to stare at one another, and that is part of the falling-into-the-bathtub for most of us.

Giving time, things, physical love, exchanging thoughts, gifts, fluids—all of these things add warm water.

How can you tell if you are adding enough warm water? You need to pay attention to how you feel. And you need to know how your spouse feels. If you both are warm and want to stay, you are adding enough. If one of you is tempted to leave, the water is too cold.

Tell the person what you appreciate about them and why you like being with them. When your actions toward the person demonstrate the respect and consideration you have for how they feel, things have a better shot.

4. Overflow—do you have an overflow drain line?

Did you install one on your bathtub? Are the drain lines plugged? Can you open the drain, or is something on it? Are you worried that if you open the drain, you'll lose your jewelry down it?

Why do you want to avoid overflowing the bathtub? Isn't warm water flowing all around and onto the floor a good thing? Really, no. The water overflowing is when you don't let things drain out, and it is really overwhelming. People can drown in a room that doesn't let the water out. I've seen people try this; they float up into the room, the bathtub fills up, the room fills up, sometimes the floor of the house gets pretty full. Sometimes people leave when their heads are near the ceiling and they can barely breathe. But leaving this way is scary—you have to duck down under water and find the bathroom door, which is sealed. You have to pry away the plastic that sealed it and open the door. Leaving is very dramatic too. The door lets the water out in a rush, and normally, lots of things that were floating around are swept out the door. It can happen fast and be pretty scary.

Draining water is really letting things go, getting over the past.

The warm water is a result of actions/thoughts in the past and hope for the future. Letting the water overflow or splashing water on the floor will eventually rot the foundation that the bathtub sits on.

When you realize that the floor beneath

your bathtub is rotten, then you may consider remodeling. Some folks do this themselves: they go to the hardware store and buy books on bathroom construction. Some folks hire to get it done: they get out of the bathtub and have a professional come in to fix the floor.

5. Learn how to drain water.

How do you let go of the past? What does it mean to actually forgive? How do you forget? Sometimes you don't. Sometimes you can't. But what happens when you cling to grievances?

Perhaps an example will help. There was a woman whose husband bought his wife flowers for her birthday. The thing was, they were having a lot of financial problems, and she wanted him to save money to pay their bills. So rather than being happy, she was mad. This is a little thing, and so they fought. She said that he wasn't listening to her. He said that he would do it again. "Your birthday needs to be celebrated. I didn't spend lots of

money, and next month, we won't even remember where we were in our saving, but you'll remember your birthday."
This did not make her happy either. She said, "When you take our money and you spend it on things we don't need, you make me feel like I am alone in this. I feel like you don't care about paying off our bills and that we will be in debt forever. Every little bit counts. It is the little things that add up, and then, we could be paid off."

They didn't agree. This argument came up over and over in their relationship. You can recognize it as the time that she bought another pair of shoes or when he let the kids have ice cream at 10:00 PM. Whenever it wasn't a joint decision, they had the opportunity for conflict. Would they read each other's minds and then passively go along with what the other person wanted? Doesn't that have its cost?

So what was to be done? Some people recounted the other person's lack of judgment to all of their family and friends.

Some people tried to control all of the decisions.

Some people tried to convince their partner of the rightness of their viewpoint and the values behind their logic.

What worked?
(This takes two people to work.)

1. Letting the other person know how you feel.
2. Letting it go. It happened. It was in the past.
3. If something similar happened again, treat it like a new incident.
4. Work toward a perspective that honors both individuals. How can you both win? What is a balance that would hold?

What didn't work?
Shrieking, nagging, and yelling.

As I write this, I have to admit that I think it is just that love overcomes these things. It is the ratio of love to the severity and frequency of the incidents. If you have enough love and the incidents are either not severe or infrequent, you will stay together happily.

If you stop making love, then it is only a matter of time until there isn't enough love to cover the incidents. One of you will leave.

If you make love often and passionately, some people think that others will forgive anything. It isn't true. Love cannot cure disrespect or real hurt.

Love provides grace to smooth over the little cracks and to ride into the next day. Love does not cover the earthquake. Love doesn't cover the mudslide.

People whose world is shaking or sliding need to address the reality of the situation and get to safety.

Safety is a higher personal value than love.

Not that we want to survive alone, but that we want to survive. Even if it means being alone.

And who is really alone? Are we not all on the same whirling earth, traveling through time together?

The message here is that we use love to cover the mistakes, and we talk about what bothers us. Like when your child stumbles when they walk. We talk about looking where we are going. Not taking too big of steps. Parents work with their children through the lessons of life.

Love and be thankful for it. Let go of the little things and start each day with a clean slate. Start with an even-point system, and try to be a blessing to the other person. If you can make them feel warm, they will most likely be kind to you. If they are not, talk with them about it. Try to listen to what they say. Get someone else to help if you just cannot hear them.

How do people do this? You've seen it

done millions of times. It is when the person laughs and says "Yes, sometimes I find that annoying, but I love him/her anyway. I realize that it is the same characteristic that I find both annoying and endearing. I just love him/her." That is said by someone who has forgiven and is living in the present rather than the past.

What do you hear when someone is unable to let go? A list of complaints and a constant airing, repetitively, of past hurts. Sometimes all we hear is silence. The person who can't let go will hold the hurt/complaints inside and let it poison their system.

6. When ice chunks fall into your tub, huddle together. Ice chunks, ice flows, stalactites—these all happen at odd times. Imagine you are sitting with your loved one, happily or unhappily, letting time go by, and then, *BAM!*

Right into your bathtub drops a huge chunk of ice.

Sometimes you are whispering in the other person's ear when this happens. If you are sitting very close and whispering in their ear, the ice will startle you, and you will crouch very close together. You may talk about how the water is getting colder. You may even try to push the ice back a bit—to the other side of the bathtub.
Sometimes someone will try to pick it up and throw it out.

You are lucky if you are together in the icy water. Two people together have a chance of keeping each other a little warm. At least one can be on the icy side, and then you can switch places.

Trouble is, sometimes the ice falls and you are on opposite sides of the bathtub. Then the water gets cold. You may not even discuss it. Sometimes there is so much ice that you can't even see your partner on the other side of it.

And it is cold.

The Bathtub

So people tend to hug themselves and cry.

It gets colder. And colder.

When it gets cold enough, people get out. If you want to find your partner in your freezing bathtub, you have to leave your warm spot, get closer to the ice, and get past the ice to the person on the other side.

It takes a lot of courage to do that.

Sometimes people try, but it is so cold that they give up and go back to their side of the tub. And of course, it isn't still warm there either.

This can be an illness, an accident, a death, or all of these.

If my child dies, that is a block of ice crashing into my bathtub. I get so cold with the huge block of ice. If my partner is on the other side of the ice, then we will both freeze. In my anger, I may even blame my spouse for my child's death. I feel cold and alone and may decide that it is too awful and that I need to get out of the bathtub.

You can see that if I am in a relationship that doesn't recognize divorce, this will take different form than if I am open to divorce. This is where folks work through counseling and, sometimes successfully, get back together on one side of the ice block. Sometimes, they learn either to thaw the ice (this is accepting the death and celebrating the life that the person did live, perhaps growing into an appreciation for the time they had with that child rather than the pain of the realization of what they don't have) or, sometimes, to put a partition in the bathtub so that they have a warm spot and the ice is on the other side of the partition. (This can be crowded, but people feel close together, and it can be warmer than just sitting by the ice. This practically looks like moving on where they don't talk about that child; the child's stuff is locked away, and folks try not to mention or think about that child.)

Sometimes, people divorce to move on. They will grow apart and try to forget.

7. Don't let anyone add burning hot water (if you can help it).

What is water that is so hot it burns? water that hurts? Water is so hot that it burns when it makes a person move when it hits them. You can tell when people feel this because they cannot stand still. They instinctively move. Just like when someone touches a hot stove and they bring their hand back really fast. Burning water does the same thing.

Burning water is things like ruining financial debt, bringing in someone else to sleep with, physical abuse.

Physical abuse can be burning or it cannot. Sometimes the victim wants to stay with the abuser because it is what they know or their love is greater than the hurt. This can be very hard for the other

The Bathtub

folks that love the victim. You can tell her to leave him, but she may not or she may take him back. Folks sometimes think this comes from poor self-esteem. Maybe so. Sometimes what holds people together in the bathtub is that they have a common dream or vision of their future. This can be very simple—a moment they see together. One I heard of was they would live in the mountains; he would chop wood, and she would read a book in a hammock. This was just a moment-dream. A moment-dream is something that can hold a couple together even when things aren't going well or if things get really ugly. A moment-dream doesn't have depth or reality; it is just a vision of a moment of them together. It can be a picture from the past, but that is easier to give up. We can all see that we don't look the same as that person in the photograph. Harder still is giving up a moment-vision of the future that is holding your soul.

It can be harder to give up the dream than the relationship with the other person.

It can take longer too.

How do you stop someone from adding burning water? Participate and know what is going on. Share your plans and thoughts so that you are making the gamble together, that it is a joint decision (when you can).

8. What about when someone you love rages at the universe (or worse, at you)?

Raging at the universe: This happens all the time. Why did God allow this to happen? Why did it keep raining? Why doesn't it rain? Why did I get caught speeding? Why did the light change just then? Why did I lose my job? How am I going to pay the bills? What do I do?

Raging at you: You are stupid! You are lazy! You are not who I want! You should have done it differently! You should have known better! You caused my problem! I am mad that this happened!

Sometimes this raging is constant, and we call it negativity or verbal abuse. Sometimes this raging leads to physical abuse.

Sometimes it does not.

Some people feel that if they are yelled at, they will leave. Some kids feel this way when their parents yell at them. They hate all the yelling and screaming. Normally, the parents' intentions are good, but they just come across as having a lack of self-control. Behaving with no self-control does not bring you respect.

The perception that being overweight is lack of self-control has killed a few marriages. People do not tend to look the same through their lifetime. Folks gain weight and lose weight. Sometimes it is because of a disease or illness. Things happen. How we react to them is pretty much determined by how we see them.

Whose fault do we think it is? Do we think the other person could have prevented it or is doing it on purpose? Do we see it as a control issue? When one spouse wants the other to change what they are doing, what is behind that? Whether it is how they spend money or whether they go to church or what they wear or eat or what the kids are allowed to know or see or do—the list of these potential issues is long.

So how do couples work through an issue? Or does everyone else just agree?

You should realize that not everyone else just agrees over things. How issues are resolved makes a big difference in the length of time the couple stays together.

9. Some people just don't look at divorce as an option.

They may stay together miserably for years. *Needs unmet.* They may accept who they married. *Needs met through others—friends, sometimes other lovers.* There's agreement that they are not the only folks in the universe.

They may figure out how to get the other person to meet their needs. *Needs met through a lifetime of negotiation and compromise* or, said better, "making it through the hard times, and the hard times made us stronger."

The thing about this is that you are still in the bathtub. You may feel alone, but the other person is in it with you. You may think it is impossible to feel warm again or to trust this person. You may think it is just not workable to understand this person. Or you may think that you have the answers, you know that this person is not who you want, not who you thought they would be, not what you need. The problem is that people change. You change and the other person changes, and life brings situations that are difficult. So when the going gets tough, what do you do?

A lot of us were taught not to accept compromise. Have you heard of people that say "No compromise"? This can translate into excellent moral ground or just selfishness or the ability to only look at one side of an argument. Sometimes it takes something that looks a lot like compromise to stay together at one end of the tub.

Our political world is full of these kinds of debates. People on one side versus people on the other side. What is the right answer? The right answer is to try to make it work and to know when to leave. That doesn't seem to say one thing, does it? So perhaps some examples would help. But perhaps not. The reality is that you have to have the right information.

What are the issues? (There are likely more than one.)
How severe are the issues? (Life, safety, trust, vow-breaking, lifestyle choices, disrespect)

Whenever folks look at their situation and decide that they are cold, alone, and don't like where they are, some folks take action. If they are open to divorce, they tend to leave and say that it is better than staying in that freezing bathtub. It works well when both people get out of the bathtub. If one stays in the freezing cold, then it makes folks sad to see it.

When do you know if you should leave? The best answer to this is to try to make it work. If you can't make it work, then leave. I have seen couples work through substance abuse and money issues. I haven't seen anyone successfully work through physical violence. I have seen unhappy people leave and actually find true love. I have seen angry people that are still angry, just in a new relationship.

The real answer is that it takes two people to have a problem. Either you have different expectations or different goals or different needs. If you can realize what part of the problem is because of who you are and what part of the problem is because of who your partner is, then you have a better chance of either solving the problem(s) or, at least, moving past your part of the problem.

If you bring your part of the problem to your next relationship, you are likely to just repeat the same stuff.

Perhaps you don't know how to add warm water. Then your next bathtub will get cool. Hopefully, you learn to add warm water. But if you are going to learn this, why not just do it with your first partner, your first marriage? Why wait for your second to learn this?

Or maybe you can't let anything go. So your first bathtub overflowed, the floor rotted, and you just had to get out before the bathtub fell through the floor. Why not fix the floor, get back in the bathtub, and learn to let the water out before it overflows?

If you move on to another relationship and you still can't let any water out, it will just happen again to you.

There are so many people that cannot see their part of the issue that they repeat their problems, and this gives divorce a bad name. Who sees this? Our kids. Kids learn and watch. They will see the repeating problems. They will see that you aren't perfect. They will blame you for not growing into who you could be, the person that can add warm water and open the drain. They will vow not to do what you are doing. They will not be kind when you are old and bitter.

Kids also see when one spouse is left in the bathtub. They hear how cold that person is, how much they miss the warm bathtub, and how they blame the person who left. They will see the person who left and whether that person just repeated the same thing. They will judge you.

Of course, not all couples have kids. If you don't have kids, then the judgment is the same; it is just that no one may voice it. There is no one to whom that may occur, except you may know it in your heart in the future years. People experience this as regret.

10. Staying together for the kids?

The marriage is the two of you, but when you have children, they learn a lot about life from your bathtub. They normally get to watch both sides of the evolution through time. So they will know if someone got out of the bathtub and someone stayed in.

If your bathtub is cold and you learn to warm it up and you stay together, then the cold bathtub was just a hard time that made your marriage stronger because you learned a skill that you needed to make any marriage work.

If your bathtub is in danger of falling through the floor and you get help to fix the floor or you fix it yourself, then that too made your marriage stronger. You have a remodeled bathroom.

However, if you are in boiling water and you leapt out of the tub, you have to either leap in and out or figure out how to stop the boiling water from being added to your tub. People get burned. Children get burned. These burns can take a long time to heal.

11. Homework

Finally, please consider this info to be a starting point. Hopefully, you can discuss your bathtub with the folks around you and get the insight you need to move positively in your life.

Typical discussion starters:

I feel like our bathtub is cold. Does it feel cold to you?

Can you _____ (fill in the blank with "stop splashing," "drain some water," or "add some warm water") to make me feel comfortable?

I've been trying _____ to make the bathtub feel better to you, is it working? What else can we do?

Appendix

My personal story

I tried to make my first marriage work for eight years. Divorce was difficult for me because I was raised Catholic, with a belief that marriage was designed by God to teach me lessons in life that I needed to learn.

So when my spouse used drugs and preached tolerance, I tried to find meaning for me. I thought I could show forgiveness and see how unconditional love could solve behavior problems.

Didn't I marry for better or for worse, in sickness and in health? So when my spouse threatened to kill me and was insane and wouldn't take medication, I learned that I cannot control other people. I had no control. I heard the message "Take care of your children and yourself."

I tried tough love—kick him out and deliver real consequences. That did not inspire him to be a part of the family in a constructive way.

I learned that being a single mom is scary, and sometimes, I would choose to stay in an abusive relationship. People said, "Get out," and "Are you and your kids okay?" People were inspired to quit drugs by watching my spouse. It scared them. Watching a bipolar person in a violent manic episode is scary.

I was self-righteous and believed that all children need time with their father. I believed this until his therapist told me that after ten years of treating children and counseling adults for another ten years, his recommendation was that sometimes children just need visits with their father.

Sometimes the example is not a good one, and limited exposure is actually healthier.

I went to therapy and was diagnosed with post-traumatic stress disorder from living with someone who threatened my safety every day.

I went to victim's services and read a poster that described an abusive relationship and realized that I had experienced typical abusive behavior.

I listened to Alcoholics Anonymous Advice to Wives. When I kept my problems a secret, I lived in isolation I **needed to share my life, to tell people at lunch, to continue talking to my sisters and friends, and to work on my understanding even when I was ashamed of what was occurring.**

I prayed. I thought that if this was my destiny, then please help me make something of it. I resented the free time and movie-watching my spouse had in the mental institution. I was always working. He had seen every new movie.

I visited my spouse in the mental institution and tried to talk to an insane person. I watched the inability to form coherent thought. I went home and cried.

I learned about court-ordered medication for attempted suicide. I paid medical bills. I dealt with the excessive spending that happened before institutions. Before jail.

I called 911 and helped the police locate my spouse.

And I lived.

Divorce.

Rather than telling you the story of my divorce, I'll share the

The Bathtub

questions I pondered for the next five years.

Did I abandon an ill person?
What was my moral obligation?
Does providing a safe environment for my children outweigh my obligation to my spouse?
What about in sickness or in health?
Did I deserve a new relationship?
Was it also my problem?
What did I contribute to the failure of my marriage?
How could I not have seen this?
Could I trust my judgment of other people?
Do you ever really know what another person will do?
Do you ever really know anyone?
Should I live alone?
Could I learn to trust?
What was my purpose in life?
Could I just enjoy the short moments of happiness and endure the rest?
Was I taking my health for granted?
How do I raise a teenage son without a father?
Should I change my name back?
Was I never going to have the complete family of my dreams?

These questions, and others, led me to share my thoughts and ideas in the beginning of this book.

Then I spent another four years wandering in search of my answers and found them.

I remarried nine years after my divorce. I am still learning. This marriage has helped me to add the last section of this book, which talks about how to add warm water and what the skills look like.

Working for a better tomorrow helps me to enjoy today.

The Bathtub

Reference Table

To prevent FAILURE	Do this in your MARRIAGE	Think of it like a BATHTUB
Natural cooling of water	Do things that make your spouse feel good. What makes you both comfy? Be nice. Do things you enjoy. Smile. Look into their eyes.	Add warm water
Rotting of the floor	Let things go / forgive.	Drain the water.
	Work on issues that bother you. Calmly. Together.	Mop up the water.
	Avoiding issues just delays failure, it is like →	Tiptoeing around the tub.
	Go to a marriage counselor; learn, make new agreements; repair the foundation if needed. Make a decision to release the old frustrations and start new. Let yourselves start again.	Hire someone to remodel your bathroom and fix the floor. Learn to drain the water and mop up the floor. Start doing both.
	Talk, read books, work on it together; learn, make new agreements. Talk when things don't work. Make changes until they do work. Try things. Think about it.	Fix-it-yourself. Go to the store and buy new flooring. Take it apart, put the new stuff in. Clean the dust, paint.
Unfair Division of Labor	Explain how you feel. Both people typically have to do all these tasks to make it work well.	Add warm water, drain the water, mop the floor.
Playing around	Don't flirt with others or think about an affair, even just in jest.	Splashing water on the floor

	Don't cheat	Sawing through the structural beams under the bathroom. Sometimes this is all it takes to make the bathtub fall through the floor and break.
	Forgive the person for cheating. Figure out what was going on. Why did they do it? What do you need to do to feel safe? Rebuild trust. Start again.	Go down to the floor below the bathroom. Add a metal support to hold up the ends of the beam where they were cut.
Ice dumped in the water	When you have a tragedy and/or a loss, you need to whisper closely to the other person how sad it makes you feel. Share what you are going through. Be together, not apart. Face it together. If you blame your partner, bring that blame with you and huddle together against the cruel world.	People who huddle together at one end of the tub stay together. If when the ice comes and you are at each end of the tub, one will have to cross to the other. IF you stay apart, it is just too cold to stay in the bathtub.
Hot water dumped in	When something happens that requires immediate decisions and actions, take the action. Focus and fix the problem. Be conservative and get help if you need it. Ask for help.	Move everyone to one side. Get out temporarily if you have to. Take the action to cool the water back to warm. Burns take time to heal.
Write in your own here:		

CPSIA information can be obtained at www.ICGtesting.com
Printed in the USA
LVOW040901161111

255241LV00002B/86/P